W9-BCT-949

How Things Get Done

How Things Get Done

*The Nitty-Gritty of
Parliamentary Procedure*

by
DENA CITRON BANK

With a Foreword by Solomon Blatt, Sr.

UNIVERSITY OF
SOUTH CAROLINA PRESS

Copyright © University of South Carolina 1979
Copyright, 1951, by Helen Kohn Hennig and Dena Citron Bank

Published in Columbia, South Carolina, by the
University of South Carolina Press, 1979

Revised Edition of *Chats on Parliamentary Procedure* by
Helen Kohn Hennig and Dena Citron Bank

Manufactured in the United States of America

First printing, hardcover, 1979

Second printing, paperback, 1980

Library of Congress Cataloging in Publication Data

Bank, Dena Citron, 1912–
  How things get done.

  Published in 1951 under title: Chats on parliamentary procedure, by H. K. Hennig and D. C. Bank.
  Includes index.
  1. Parliamentary practice.   I. Hennig, Helen Kohn. Chats
on parliamentary procedure.   II. Title.
JF515.B24   1979   060.4 2   79–1287
ISBN 0-87249-343-1

Contents

Foreword

IT IS A GREAT PLEASURE for me to heartily commend Dena Citron Bank's little manual on how to make sense of parliamentary procedure. Its remarkable merit, it seems to me, is that experience with previous versions of it have shown that Dena has an extraordinary ability to make the rudiments of parliamentary procedure clear to people—lots of people. And that's important because when you don't understand the rules of a game you can't play that game very well. People who want to change this world (which is always in need of a certain amount of changing) are often frustrated because they haven't mastered those basic principles by which things get done in a democracy; they sometimes become bitter and apocalyptic when they'd make a lot more headway if they sat down and read *How Things Get Done* from cover to cover and then read it from cover to cover again. You can read it in less than an hour. It could change your life.

Parliamentary procedure varies slightly from one place to another and from one organization to another, of course. Most modern legislatures, for instance, have added their own wrinkles to the classic principles that Robert elaborated. But the basic ground rules are what this book summarizes so neatly, and *those* are what you really need to know if you want to get your point of view across to people in any deliberative assembly, whether it be the Worldwide Committee to Preserve *Homo sapiens* or your local group of orchid-growers.

> Solomon Blatt, Sr.
> Speaker Emeritus,
> The House of Representatives
> of the General Assembly
> of the State of South Carolina
> and its Speaker for Thirty-three years.

Preface

IF YOU CAN RIDE a bicycle or swim or drive a car, you can learn as much as you're ever likely to need to know about parliamentary procedure. Once you've managed to swim a few feet or drive a car around the block, you never really lose the technique, and once you've mastered the fundamentals of parliamentary procedure you'll never again find yourself sitting through a meeting in bewilderment because you can't pick the thread of common sense out of what's happening.

The basic principles of conducting meetings in the United States today are those that were codified by Henry Martyn Robert in 1876 and I recommend that you use an up-to-date edition of *Robert's Rules of Order* as your authority whenever what I've written here isn't complete enough to settle a procedural problem. You shouldn't need it very often, but it's good to have it there when you do need it. Every organization needs to own a copy. Ask the best bookseller in town to get the latest complete edition for your group.

Robert, by the way, was an interesting character. He was born in South Carolina in 1837, in a little town so full of his kinfolk it was called Robertville. He graduated from West Point in 1857. When the Civil War came he was one of those officers who remained at his post in the United States Army. Quiet, methodical, and extremely conscientious, he must have felt a tangle of loyalties when he found himself at war with his homeland but he pursued his duties as a military engineer and worked on the defenses of Philadelphia, Washington, and the coast of New England. When you think of someone as a military engineer, your first thought is not likely to be of someone rising at a meeting to address the chair, but think again: the design and construction of military defenses must have involved a good deal of consultation between civilians and soldiers and the engineers probably found themselves mediating between both. And Henry M. Robert noticed that such meetings often resulted in confusion and disappointment for all concerned because there were no generally accepted rules of procedure to follow. So he compiled the best set of procedures he could come up with and after several years of use, in 1876, by which time he had reached the rank of Colonel, they were published as *A Pocket Manual of Rules of Order for Deliberative Assemblies*. So there you are: in case you didn't know, what you are likely to join is a deliberative assembly. Colonel Robert was Brigadier General Robert by the time he retired, so we may assume that he was a very effective coordinator of meetings. He was still alive in 1915 when his work finally acquired its modern name: *Robert's Rules of Order Newly Revised*.

He did not, of course, *invent* the rules of parliamentary procedure. He drew on a large body of opinion and practice, especially the manual of parliamentary law that Thomas Jefferson compiled when he was presiding over the United States Senate. And Jefferson's own set of rules was largely derived from the practice of the British House of Commons.

I'm not writing a textbook, but it will do you no harm as you go through my book to remember that the basic procedures of debate and discussion have been tested by centuries of experience. They go back to the early days of the House of Commons in thirteenth-century England and they have been found to produce the best compromise available between two alternatives. Those two alternatives are:

1. A frenzy in which everybody speaks and no one is heard.
2. A ritual in which everybody finds themselves accepting, whether they like it or not, the dictates of a few.

That, my friends, is what parliamentary procedure saves us from, and the "rules" are really no more than a time-honored agreement that we'll all drive on the same side of the road.

It's a curious thing that *Robert's Rules*, compiled by a Southerner who fought for the Union, are now the standard authority for groups and debating societies not only throughout the United

States but to a large degree throughout the English-speaking world. So if the rules don't seem sensible at first, learn them and try them: you'll find they work. But, if you happen to have any members of your club who are used to the way things are done in England, you'd best be sure they understand that when we *table a motion* we mean exactly the opposite of what the English mean: we mean to cut off debate indefinitely; in England the phrase refers to *opening* debate, not closing it.

One final word of advice: read *all* of this little book, from beginning to end. You don't have to remember it all, but when you've read it through once you'll have an idea how the pieces fit together. When a particular problem comes up, you can then turn to these pages for help, but things will go much better if you already know a bit about the pages you're turning. In short, don't wait until you're sick before you find yourself a doctor: make the acquaintance of the doctor first—and then maybe you won't get sick.

It is important that *every* member of an organization understand the rules of parliamentary procedure. A successful meeting is the reponsibility of the presiding officer, the other officers, and the committee chairmen, but most of all it is the responsibility of everyone who attends the meeting.

My own jobs as a medical and psychiatric social worker involved me in meetings of various community groups, and I soon found that I needed to sort out for myself the nitty-gritty of conducting a meeting. With Helen Kohn Hennig as my mentor, I became Parliamentarian of the Woman's Club of Columbia, South Carolina, who in 1951 published a booklet by Helen and myself entitled *Chats on Parliamentary Procedure. How Things Get Done* is a slightly expanded version of that publication and has been updated with the benefit of my experience in teaching the subject. Drafts of it have been used by many different organizations, some of them all male, some of them all female, some of them mixed. I find "Chairperson," "Committee person," "Congress person," "Spokesperson," etc. contrived and awkward, so I have used "Mr. Chairman," "Madam Chairman," "The Chair," and "The Presiding Officer," as the case may be.

Cordially, Dena Citron Bank

Columbia, South Carolina, *November 15, 1978*

How Things Get Done

Some DOs
and DON'Ts

DO Address the chair by title (Mister President, Madam President, Madam Chairman, Mister Chairman) not by name, and under no circumstances by a person's given name.

DO Stand when presiding over business.

DO Remember to call for the negative vote and declare the result of all votes.

DO Know the constitution of your club and abide by it—most constitutions differ.

DO Keep order at all times and under all circumstances.

DO Start meetings at the appointed hour, with no waiting for stragglers.

DO Ask for discussion on a debatable motion.

DO Be sure that the Credentials Committee (used in conventions) states the voting strength.

DO Establish that a quorum is present in order to avoid embarrassment later.

DO Use every effort to limit business sessions to one hour.

DO See that your club adopts some standard parliamentary authority, such as *Robert's Rules of Order.*

DO Have all accounts of the club audited—as a matter of course.

DO Secure for all equal rights of speech, participation, and leadership.

————————————

DON'T Discuss business unless it has been introduced by motion or resolution.

DON'T Read board minutes at a general meeting, but do read minutes to the group that made them.

DON'T Talk to your neighbor; all conversation must be directed to the chair and through it to others at the meeting.

I. Call to Order

Every meeting must have an order of business, sometimes called the "agenda." The way in which a business meeting is begun is as follows: The president, or the presiding officer, stands, *strikes once firmly* with the gavel, and says, "The meeting will please come to order." After that the meeting begins and everyone, that means every single person at the meeting, comes to order and is quiet. No one continues conversation. It is exceedingly important that meetings be called to order on time, not one minute before nor one minute after the hour. Do not wait for stragglers. If they know you are going to wait for them, they will continue to be stragglers. It may work a hardship at first, but soon the members will learn that the meeting will start at the hour at which it was called.

II. Quorums

The question of conducting business often hinges on a "quorum." Usually the quorum, that is the number of people necessary for the conduct of business, is set in the organization's by-laws. It should be kept reasonable, usually a percentage of the membership. However, if it is not so stipulated, a majority of the entire membership usually constitutes a quorum. (For further interpretation see *Robert*.)

III. Motions

It is necessary to introduce the business of a meeting through what we call a motion, or through communications, reports, or resolutions. If the business is introduced through the last three methods mentioned, then a motion must be made in order to bring some action before the body. The correct wording is "I move to" or "I move that." There are various types of motions and only those most often used will be considered in this book. The first is called a main motion. A main motion is something which introduces business. For instance, "Mister Chairman, I move that we hold this class for five consecutive days." That is a motion and, after it has been seconded and stated by the chair, it would be open for discussion. (The matter of so-called "privileged motions" will be considered a little later.)

We wish to stress that a motion is always necessary before any matter may be considered by a meeting. If, when a letter requiring action is read a motion is not made, then information in that letter simply hangs suspended. For instance, you have a letter of resignation from an individual. The secretary reads the letter of resignation. If that is all, the individual has not resigned, or at least the body has not accepted or refused to accept the resignation. The reading of the letter must be followed by a motion which might be stated in this manner: "Mister Chairman, I move that the resignation of so-and-so be accepted with regret." After the motion is seconded, discussion takes place on the motion, and then the matter is either voted down or voted for. If no such motion has been made, the letter would simply have been read.

How to Make a Motion Certain formalities must be observed in presenting a motion. First, you must secure the floor. How does one secure the floor? By rising and addressing the presiding officer by official title, either "Mister/Madam Chairman," "Mister/Madam President," "Mister/Madam Presiding Officer," or whatever the official recognized title is. (Do not raise or wave your hand for recognition.) Then wait for recognition. This waiting for recognition is a sign to the presiding officer that you are asking quietly (and according to parliamentary procedure) for the privilege of saying something. What that something may be is usually a motion. Then the presiding officer turns to the member and says, "Mr. Jones" or "Mrs. Smith." If the presiding officer does not know the name of the person who is asking for recognition he may look at that person and

nod approval for the member to speak. It is cour-
teous for the member to present his or her own
name if the member sees the presiding officer is
embarrassed. In many organizations presenting
your name is required for the records so that the
secretary, or the stenotypist, or whoever is taking
the official record, may be sure to get your name
properly recorded.

Suppose that more than one person rises and
asks for the floor at the same time. It is the duty
of the presiding officer to recognize the person
who rose first and addressed the chair. If the addressing of the chair came simultaneously, then
the chair must recognize the one who, it seems to
the presiding officer, had first choice of the right
to speak. (Of course, if a presiding officer makes
a decision, and the body itself does not feel that it
is a fair decision, they can "appeal from the decision of the chair" and vote on whether to sustain
the chair (see pages 63–64). A vote must then be
taken. However, this probably will not happen
very often in the organizations in which you are
a member.) Having been recognized by the chair,
the person who wants to present the motion does
so in these words: "Madam Chairman, *I move*

that we have a picnic next Friday," or "Mister Chairman, *I move that* we continue this class." Whatever the motion may be, the form in which you say it is, "I move that" or "I move to." Please do not say "I motion that we do so-and-so," or even that "I make a motion." The correct form is "I move."

SECONDING THE MOTION   It is necessary in most instances (we shall not at this time consider the variations) to have a second to the motion. That means that another person in the membership agrees to bring the matter to the body for discussion. If you second a motion, it does not necessarily mean that you are in favor of that motion. You may simply second it in order to get it on the floor for discussion, because most matters of business must be moved and seconded before they may be considered by the body. The form which you use in seconding the motion is "I second the motion." Then it is the duty of the chair (that is, the presiding officer) to state the motion as it has been presented and seconded. After that the chair asks for discussion, and the discussion must be orderly. Members talk to the chair—they do not talk to each other—rise and ask for permission to discuss the matter. Then, when there is no further discussion, the chair calls for a vote.

AFFIRMATIVE AND NEGATIVE VOTES When the vote is taken the presiding officer must always be very careful to call for both the affirmative and the negative vote. This is important even if every single member of the organization votes for the motion, because the chair must be able (legally) to say that both the affirmative and the negative votes have been called for. The form in which the chair announces the vote is as follows: "It appears to the chair that the 'ayes' have it and the motion is carried." If the vote is against the motion, if more persons vote "no" than "yes," then the form used by the chair to announce the vote is, "It appears to the chair that the 'noes' have it and the motion is lost." Whatever the outcome of the vote, it is imperative that the chair announce the result of the vote. The chair must announce the vote and must be sure to call for both the "ayes" and the "noes." (Some presiding officers do not call for the "noes," which is bad procedure.)

May we insert a word here to members. You don't always have to vote "yes." It is perfectly possible and perfectly proper for you to vote "no." In fact, it is much better for you to vote a motion down at a meeting when the matter is being considered than it is to vote for it and then go out and criticize your own action. Remember that you are free to vote "yes" or "no" according to the way you feel about the business being considered.

STATING THE MOTION   It is usually required that the presiding officer state the motion on which a vote is being taken. The presiding officer must state the motion exactly as the maker of the motion put it, not as the chair thinks it should have been stated. This is important, because the very stating of the motion on which the vote is being taken often influences the voter in one direction or another. It is not fair for the presiding officer to change the meaning or intent of the motion presented by someone else. Frequently, it is required that the maker of a motion write the motion out and present it either to the secretary or to the presiding officer. If that is to be done, it is important that it be done at the time the motion is offered.

Written copies of motions are quite good form, but should be required at the time the motion is made.

BASIC RULES   Although there are many exceptions to these rules, a few fundamental basic rules may make this matter of presenting and considering motions easier. Here they are: The general rules of parliamentary procedure say that

1. No motion may be made without a quorum being present;
2. Any motion duly offered under the proper conditions by a member must be considered;
3. A member must have the floor to make or second a motion;
4. Every main motion before being considered must be seconded;
5. Most motions may be amended, debated, and reconsidered; and
6. Most motions may be decided by majority vote.

Those are the basic rules. There are many exceptions which just make things more interesting. (See pages 81–85.)

SOME EXCEPTIONS   There are some exceptions
to the basic rules. The two principal ones are the
following:

1. No quorum is necessary when a motion is
made to adjourn or to fix the time or place to
which to adjourn, as "I move that we adjourn until tomorrow morning at 9 o'clock in this hall," or
to take a recess.

2. Any member who makes a motion has a
right to have it considered except if the motion
has nothing to do with the organization.

Let's say that in a meeting we had a motion
that the United Nations should spend a billion
dollars this year on organizing social welfare
units. We have nothing to do with the United Nations or how it spends its money. The only things
we could do would be to move that this group
send a communication to the United Nations, but
we would not have the right of spending their
money as an act approved by this group. The
matter of consideration or appropriateness of
consideration may also be raised, and if it is considered inadvisable to study the problem at that

particular moment, the motion may be set aside until some later date or later hour.

For other exceptions see pages 81–85.

MOTIONS MOST FREQUENTLY USED   A list of motions, which is about to be presented to you, should be memorized.

Motions for Ready Reference

When any motion in this list is pending, the motion above it is in order; any below are out of order.

12. To fix the time to which to adjourn
11. To adjourn
10. To raise a question of privilege
9. To adopt the orders of the day
8. To table (or take from the table) a motion
7. To call for the previous question
    (to close debate)
6. To postpone to a specified time
5. To commit or to refer to committee
4. To amend the amendment

3. To amend
2. To postpone indefinitely
1. To make the main motion

We are assuming now that the (1) main motion has been introduced; that is, someone has risen, addressed the chair, been recognized, and stated a motion, which in turn has been duly seconded. The first motion following the presentation of the main motion is to (3) amend. Let's be specific. The main motion has been presented and is as follows: "I move that this class continue for ten days instead of five," and that motion has been seconded. Someone rises and says, "I move to amend by substituting the words 'three weeks' for 'ten days'." That in turn is seconded. If you are going to vote on the motion, you should vote on the amendment first. In other words, you present the voting in the reverse order. The amendment is voted upon first, then the motion itself, either as amended, if the amendment passed, or as originally stated if the amendment failed. Now, this is not easy, but it is important and often leads to confusion.

In order to simplify this list of motions, we shall speak of them by rank. The first motion made is considered the lowest in rank, and the motion (12) to *fix the time or place to which to adjourn* is the highest in rank. This is always true, because a motion to *adjourn* (11 or 12) takes precedence over every other motion. We shall discuss that in more detail a little later. To return to the list. We have mentioned the main motion and the motion to amend. Now we may have a motion (4) to *amend the amendment*. To go back to our example. The motion was that we should amend by substituting the words "three weeks" for "ten days." Now someone moves to "amend the amendment" by moving to "amend by substituting 'twenty-one days' for the previous amendment of 'three weeks'." The second amendment, that is the motion to amend the amendment to the motion, is considered before the motion to amend. You see, we are still going backwards, so to speak. But suppose that the motion (5) to *commit, or to send the entire matter to a committee* is passed. Obviously, you can't send it to a committee, or ask for a report from a committee, and still move to amend by making it three weeks or even twenty-one days. The motion to commit would, if passed, for the time being at any rate, remove the matter from discussion. In that instance the entire matter for discussion would be reopened when the committee made its report.

Suppose, on the other hand, that it was decided not to send it to committee, which is the fifth motion on our list. Instead, it was decided (6) to *postpone* until the session on Friday. This would definitely set a time for consideration, and the pending motions would also be pending until that set time. The motion to *postpone indefinitely*, which is (2) on our list, has as its object the killing of the motion which is under consideration. This does not always work, because renewal of its consideration may be called at a subsequent meeting, unless there is a club rule prohibiting such action. If the motion to postpone to Friday is defeated then we would go back to vote on our third, second, and first motions, in that order.

The seventh motion, which is a call for the previous question, is discussed in detail on pages 25–30.

The eighth motion is to *lay on the table*. That is generally considered a very polite and nice way to kill the whole motion. If a motion is made to lay the entire matter on the table, and it is passed, then the rest of it, including all amendments, would all be killed automatically. Suppose, however, that in the midst of the debate, the motion (11) to *adjourn* were made. Now, because a person makes a motion to adjourn doesn't mean that you have to adjourn. That has to be voted on as does any other motion, but it does take precedence over the other motions pending, and always has the first consideration.

The twelfth motion is to *fix the time or place to which to adjourn*, and that even takes precedence over a general adjournment, because you conduct the business of the organization more efficiently if you set a time at which to come together again. It's important to remember that you always take the highest numbered motion first. Of course, this list does not include all the motions which may be made and voted upon before the main motion comes to a vote, but it does cover most of the things with which we will be concerned. For instance, if a motion to commit is made, a motion to amend the main motion could not be entertained by the chair, unless the motion to commit were first voted upon and lost. If the motion to commit were passed, then the matter would rest there.

It is well to remember that the first six of these motions are debatable, that is (1) to make the main motion, (2) to postpone indefinitely, (3) to amend, (4) to amend the amendment, (5) to commit or refer, and (6) to postpone definitely. The last six of these motions, (7) to call for the previous questions, (8) to lay on the table or to take from the table, (9) to adopt the orders of the day, (10) to raise a question of privilege, (11) to adjourn, or (12) to fix the time or place to which to adjourn, are not debatable. That means simply, that when any of the last six motions are made you may not discuss them. Almost all motions are discussable or debatable. These six are not.

Eleven of these twelve motions are carried by a simple majority vote. Number 7, the "previous question," requires a two-thirds vote. The first, third, fifth, sixth, and twelfth can be amended. It is wise to remember, also, that only two motions to amend may be pending at any one time, and that the second motion to amend must be a motion to amend the proposed amendment.

MOTIONS TO AMEND Motions to amend must be germane (that is, pertinent or related) to the subject of the main motion. In parliamentary procedure, as a rule, amendments which do not have anything to do with the subject of the main motion are not entertained although in some legislative halls so-called "bobtail" bills can be introduced.

When an amendment is not germane the chair makes the ruling. The presiding officer simply says, "The amendment is not germane to the main subject, therefore the chair will not entertain the amendment." Of course, that ruling in turn may be appealed from the floor.

There are several forms for amendments. We may move to amend by (1) inserting or adding; (2) by striking out or deleting; or (3) by substituting. The last mentioned amendment form is usually the most troublesome. The motion to amend by substituting may be to substitute a word, a phrase, or a clause, for some other word, phrase, or clause in a motion which we propose to amend, or by substituting an entire proposition in place of the one already submitted. Of course it has the same weight as the motion to strike out or insert. If a motion has been poorly presented it is often better to substitute an entire proposition rather than to try to change the wording, which is sometimes a very difficult thing. The usual form for amendment is "I move to amend by inserting (or adding), etc." and we might do well to memorize that little phrase, which makes the life of a presiding officer infinitely easier.

MOTIONS TO COMMIT OR REFER Motions to commit or refer, which are number 5 on our list, may be made after motions to amend have been presented, but not after any of the motions which follow in the list have been made and have not been voted upon. The usual form is, "I move to refer the question to a committee," or "I move to refer the matter to the ways and means committee," let's say. If this motion is affirmatively voted then it temporarily disposes of the main motion and any amendments that may be pending. In other words, the motion to refer cannot apply to the motion or motions to amend without including the main motion. Neither can it apply to the main motion and not include whatever amendments are pending. For instance, suppose the motion again is "I move that we continue these classes for ten days." Someone moves to amend by substituting "twenty-one days" for "ten days" and then someone moves to refer the matter to the committee on rules. Obviously, the motion is that the whole matter be referred to the committee on rules, and at this time not consider the main motion or amendments.

The motion to refer may be amended and it may be debated. For instance, the motion may be to refer to the committee on rules. That motion may be discussed or someone may offer an amendment to the effect that the entire matter be referred to the committee on procedure, or some other committee. The motion to refer to a standing committee always takes precedence over a motion to refer to a special committee. (The motion to commit or to send to a committee becomes a main motion when it is the first motion made upon the report of an officer, or a communication which has been read to the assembly.) To illustrate: suppose a president has made his report and someone moves that the report be referred to a committee on the president's message. That motion becomes a main motion as it is a way of disposing of the business suggested in the president's report.

MOTIONS TO POSTPONE DEFINITELY   There is a great difference between the motion to postpone consideration until a definite time and the motion to refer to a committee. We can imagine a situation in which a committee never reports to the group. In fact, that happens all the time in legislative bodies and is one of the things people are most annoyed about. However, the motion to postpone further consideration to a certain definite time means that the matter will be reported at the time set. This motion may be amended as to the time and may be debated. For instance, you may move, "I move to postpone the further consideration of this motion (meaning the main motion) until Thursday morning at 11 o'clock (or until the next regular meeting)." If someone feels that the matter cannot be duly considered between now and Thursday, they may move to amend by substituting the words "Thursday a week" and that is both debatable and to be voted upon. If the vote is affirmative on this motion, then the matter is temporarily disposed of until it is reported back. In other words, all the motions and amendments are held in abeyance until the matter is presented. The question which has been postponed to a set time becomes (9) an order of the day for that set time.

Under the head of "Unfinished Business" at the meeting to which consideration has been postponed, the chair announces that the postponed motion is before the assembly. Only the main motion and the motions to amend are considered as being pending. In other words, the motion to commit is not considered unless it is offered again. After all, you have postponed consideration until a specific time, and therefore, unless someone again moves to commit the matter for further study, you proceed with the discussion and the vote. The motion to commit and to postpone to a specific time may each be amended, the rules already given for amending the main motion being applicable to these.

THE PREVIOUS QUESTION (TO CLOSE DEBATE)   We now come to an often difficult, little understood, and badly misused motion, that of the previous question. Undoubtedly, much of the confusion which has arisen about this motion is due to the fact that it is badly named. It means actually, and this is of the utmost importance, "I move that all debating now cease and that we begin voting on the motion." A motion calling for the previous question may be called for the entire matter under discussion, that is, the main motion, its amendments, or its motion to commit or to postpone or various other things. If you wish to end debate on all pending motions you must say so. If, however, you wish that debate be stopped only on the question of whether to postpone to a certain time or whether to commit the matter, you so state. You would say, "I move the previous question on the motion to postpone," or "the motion to refer." Then the vote is taken only on whether you should stop debate on those particular matters. There is no discussion allowed after the call for the previous question is adopted. It is perfectly possible for someone to move the previous question before any debate is held. However, that is rather rare. This motion is generally used when a member of the group feels that the discussion has gone on long enough and everybody knows everything they need to know about the subject in order to come to a decision.

The form is very simple, but in order to avoid confusion we should drill a little on it. The question is before the house in the form of a motion and a second. Shall we demonstrate? Someone has moved that Mrs. Jones be invited to speak at our next club meeting on proposed amendments to the U.S. Constitution. That motion has been duly seconded and is before the club for discussion. Someone moves to amend by substituting Mr. Smith for Mrs. Jones, or moves to amend by adding Mr. Smith also, so that Mrs. Jones and Mr. Smith will be asked to speak. The discussion has gone on and on, and a member of the club wishes to bring it to a vote. She rises, secures the floor or the attention of the presiding officer, is recognized, and says, "Madam Chairman, I move the previous question." This requires a second. Immediately the presiding officer says (*now this is of utmost importance*): "The previous question has been moved and seconded. That means we will now vote on whether you wish to end the debate." (Many presiding officers make the serious

blunder of having the previous question moved
and then immediately presenting the motion on
which the discussion was held.)

This is technical, and to some of you may seem
difficult, so let us demonstrate. The motion before
the house is that Mrs. Jones and Mr. Smith shall
be invited to speak at the next meeting. Someone
has risen, secured the floor, and moved the previous question, which has been seconded. The
presiding officer then says, "We will vote on the
motion as to whether we shall stop debating the
question of having both Mrs. Jones and Mr. Smith
as our speakers." You do not put the vote on the
question of whether Mrs. Jones and Mr. Smith
should be asked to speak. All you vote on is
whether the group has had enough talk about it,
enough discussion, and is now ready to decide
what they want to do. In other words, when you
vote on the previous question you are simply saying "yes" or "no" to the question of whether there
has been enough discussion. If two-thirds of the
members vote "yes" then the previous question is
passed and *immediately* the presiding officer calls
for a vote on the question of whether Mrs. Jones
and Mr. Smith shall be invited to speak. There is

no further discussion possible if the body has voted to end the discussion, which is what the previous question is. If two-thirds of the members do not vote to stop discussion, it can go on indefinitely or until someone again moves the previous question, and it is carried.

Now let's review this very briefly. A motion is before the house. A discussion has taken place on the motion. Someone moves the previous question. Please do not sit in your seat and scream "question" to the chair. If you have a good presiding officer, he or she will ignore you, because you should rise, address the chair, and say "I move the previous question." Most presiding officers get very flustered and very unhappy when people in the audience remain in their seats and scream "question." It is very bad parliamentary manners. After the motion for the previous question has been presented and seconded the presiding officer says "the previous question has been called. There is no debate on this motion. We will immediately vote on the question of whether you want to stop debate. That is all you are voting on," and calls for the vote. If two-thirds of the people present vote "yes," the motion is carried and debate has been stopped. There is no question on that subject. It has been stopped, and the presiding officer calls for the vote on the question which was under discussion when "the previous question" was moved, which was, in this case, the motion that Mrs. Jones and Mr. Smith be invited to speak at the next meeting. If the previous question is lost, that is, if two-thirds of the people present do not vote for it, then the discussion may continue.

LAYING ON THE TABLE   Most people consider the motion to lay on the table as being an unfriendly motion. In other words, it is a polite way of killing the whole matter, but that is not necessarily true. It is, however, a quicker way of setting aside the main motion than to refer it to a committee or to postpone it for further consideration, because the motion to lay on the table can be neither amended nor debated. The purpose of moving that a matter be laid on the table may be to delay action to a more favorable time, or to secure time for consideration of business which is considered at that minute more urgent. The motion to lay on the table, if it is carried, that is, if it is voted for, takes from consideration of the body every motion pending on that subject, except in certain instances which will probably not come up in your experience.

ORDERS OF THE DAY Orders of the day are what the term implies, in that it means that there is an order set for the business of the day. If a special order has been set, it must be called for, but if a regular order is followed it means that matters are treated in order and with due attention to each thing. Many presiding officers seem to be uncertain of an order for business, so a suggested agenda is given.

§ *Call to Order* §

Approval of the Minutes
Report of the Treasurer
Recommendations from the Board
Corresponding Secretary's Communications
Special Orders of the Day
Reports of Standing Committees
Reports of Special Committees
Unfinished Business
New Business

Announcements

Adjournment

Program

(If there are elections of delegates or of new members, or for the filling of vacancies, that business should come between Special Orders and Reports of Committees. This does not apply to the election of officers.)

QUESTIONS OF PRIVILEGE OR PERSONAL PRIVI- LEGE A question of privilege has to do with questions respecting the personal comfort or rights of members. It is not to be confused with privileged motions. The form used is "I rise to a question of privilege," or "I rise to a question of information." The chair says, "State your question." The chair usually settles the matter or may call for a vote.

ADJOURNMENT The motion to adjourn, num- ber 11 on the list, and the motion to fix the time or place to which to adjourn, number 12 on the list, do not relate to a main motion but are consid- ered as privileged main motions. They may be acted upon at any convenient time. The state- ment is frequently made that a motion to adjourn is always in order. That is not true. It is not in order when the same motion has just been defeated nor when a motion to fix the time or place to which to adjourn is pending. As all motions have to be made after attention is granted by the presiding officer, it cannot be offered while a person is speaking or while a vote is being taken. The motion to adjourn is never debatable and cannot be amended. It must be seconded and carried by a majority vote. After the vote is taken on the motion to adjourn, the chair decides whether it has been carried or not. If it has been carried then the chair adjourns the meeting. The assembly should always remain seated until the chair has declared adjournment. Frequently just the word "adjournment" means a hasty exit of the members—very bad manners, to say the least.

When a motion to adjourn is carried and other motions are pending before the house, those motions are brought before the assembly at the next meeting under the head of "unfinished business" unless the next meeting is a specially called meeting for some particular purpose. No motion is considered as pending at a subsequent meeting except a main motion and motions to amend.

Only the members may adjourn a meeting. They may vote by "silent consent." The presiding officer would ask if there was any further business. If no further business, the chair would say, "If there is no further business, and *no objection*, the meeting is adjourned."

IV. Committees and Committee Reports

Most of the business of any organization is planned by committees, some of which are standing committees, that is, provided for in the constitution or by-laws and others are special committees appointed for one particular job. Much misinformation exists as to the power of a committee. As a matter of fact, a committee has no power except that which is specifically given to it by the club. For instance, the club may refer a matter to a committee with power to act, which is not at all unusual under such circumstances. However, if the power to act is not assigned to the committee, the committee can only study the matter and report back to the club for action.

A report of the committee should be read to the organization and should contain definite statements of information procured, duties performed, or specific recommendations showing the opinion of the committee. It should not under any circumstances be the minutes of the committee meeting, although committees are entirely at liberty to appoint a secretary and have minutes of the committee meeting checked. Frequently the committee gives only information which the organization desires. On other occasions they recommend action. The chairman generally signs the report first and the other members follow with their signatures. This is important because each signature is a guarantee to the club that the committee members are familiar with the report and thereby endorse it. Their names should be read by the person giving the report.

What do you do with a committee report after it has been rendered? If the report is only information, the chair would ask if there are any questions. If it contains recommendations for action, the chairman of the committee would move the adoption of the recommendations, and they would be considered one at a time. No second is needed since the committee has agreed on the motion to adopt. Should changes in these recommendations be desired amendments can be offered just exactly as any motion may be amended. That does not mean that the club can change the report of the committee. It can only change the action which is taken on that report.

In making a committee report it is possible that the majority of the committee may agree upon an action to be recommended, whereas the minority may not agree that that action is wise. The minority always has the right to bring in what is called a minority report, which states the views of the minority of the committee. The majority report is read first, although notice is given that the minority report is also to be heard, and action may be taken upon either or none of the reports given. Something has to be done with the reports and the recommendations. They cannot be left hanging. That is an important matter for the presiding officer to remember—that reports must be acted upon.

There is one very tricky committee about which we shall speak briefly—the *Committee of the Whole*. This was a device adopted in the days of

King James I when the House of Commons wanted to circumvent the king. They thereupon decided to become a Committee of the Whole, with the speaker and sergeant-at-arms excused. There are certain advantages in this. One, of course, being that no minutes are kept in the organization's minute book of the action taken or the speeches made in a meeting of the Committee of the Whole. It might be a wise idea to have a meeting become a Committee of the Whole when a series of resolutions or the revision of a constitution or by-laws is under consideration, because people will feel freer to express their opinions if they know every word they say is not going to be incorporated in the minutes.

The change from the regular meeting to a session of the Committee of the Whole is accomplished by having an affirmative vote taken on a motion to the effect that the meeting resolve itself into a Committee of the Whole for the purpose designated in the motion. Such a motion is in order whenever a motion to commit is in order. Should the motion prevail, the presiding officer calls someone to the chair, and takes his or her place as a member of the committee. The same quorum is required for a Committee of the Whole as is required for any meeting of the organization. The same rules apply to the Committee of the Whole that apply to other committees. They recommend to the organization whatever action they deem wise. The Committee of the Whole may consider only matters referred to it. The proper motion to close the session of any Committee of the Whole is that the committee "rise." Then they report to the president, who again resumes the chair, that the Committee of the Whole has now "risen" and is ready to make its recommendations.

V. Reports of Officers

REPORT OF THE PRESIDENT It might be well to emphasize that a president or presiding officer would not take part in debate. It is quite obvious that holding the office of president lends a great deal of prestige to what that person has to say, and it is not fair for the president to use the prestige of office to put across a point from the chair. If, at any time, a president feels that he must enter into the debate, he must get out of the chair and ask another officer to preside in his place. Under these circumstances, the president does not resume the chair until that motion has been put to a vote.

A communication from the president is read by that officer without relinquishing the chair. It is the only communication of its sort not read by one of the secretaries. Sometimes it happens that a president has exceeded his authority since the last meeting and his communication may be in the form of a report on this action and the reasons therefor. He usually asks the organization to sustain his action, and in most instances, unless there are some strong reasons to do otherwise, the assembly does sustain him.

(The motion to sustain or ratify action is a main motion and is debatable. It requires a majority vote. This motion is used when action has been taken outside of a meeting or when no quorum was present. If the motion to ratify is passed, the body assumes responsibility and pays the bills. If it is lost, the members who acted are responsible.)

REPORT OF THE CORRESPONDING SECRETARY   The corresponding secretary, or if no corresponding secretary is available, the recording secretary, reads all communications addressed to the organization except those of the president, whether from members of the organization or from organizations or individuals outside of this organization. Each communication should be acted upon before another is read. Of course, action will vary with the character of the communication. Some, such as to pay bills, may be disposed of with a simple motion acted upon; others, as on the contents of a letter, will require discussion before action. A letter of withdrawal or resignation from membership or office may be disposed of by a motion to accept the withdrawal or the resignation of the member. Communications which cannot wisely be acted upon quickly may be referred to a committee, or laid on the table, or a time may be set for deliberation of the communication.

REPORT OF THE TREASURER   The treasurer's report is usually a statement of money received and spent; obviously, it is not available for a careful audit by the members. The treasurer, after giving his report may move the acceptance of the report, which means that it will either be placed on file or made a part of the minutes. In most organizations, these reports are audited at stated intervals, and the auditor states that he finds them correct or incorrect. The fact that you accept the report of the treasurer in no way means that you accept or deny its accuracy. Establishing accuracy is entirely a matter for a careful audit.

Accepting a treasurer's report means only that you heard it. After it is read the chair may ask if there are any questions. After questions (if any) are answered, the chair will say, "If there are no questions (or further questions) the treasurer's report is accepted as information."

REPORTS OF OTHER OFFICERS   Reports of other officers are handled like committee reports. If they only give information, such reports can be accepted by silent consent. If they contain recommendations for action, a motion to adopt is in order.

"ACCEPT AND ADOPT"   *Accept* is a term usually applied to the receipt of information and does not imply any action to be taken. To *adopt* implies action, and when recommendations are adopted, action will be taken. Adopting varies from accepting a report in that accepting it implies simply receipt of information and adoption means something will happen as a result of the report. A motion to place on file is applied to a written communication or report which at that time is considered to need no further study. If a report of an officer or committee is accepted, it must of necessity either be placed on file or entered in the minutes, even though a motion to that effect has not been passed; otherwise there would be no copy of the report on which action had been taken. This is of the utmost importance, because the minutes or files are the record of all business transacted by the organization.

Sometimes a motion is made that a report or communication be entered in the minutes, which means that an effort is made to be sure that the entire manuscript appears in the permanent records of the organization. Sometimes we say we move to "spread upon the record," which is exactly the same as saying "enter in the minutes."

APPROVING THE MINUTES   To approve the minutes is the form to be used whereby the minutes become the legal record of the proceedings of any body. The minutes of every meeting should be read—unless each member has been supplied with a copy before the meeting. The question is on whether or not they should be approved, and the usual form is as follows: "You have heard the reading of the minutes. Are there any corrections, additions, or omissions? If not, the minutes stand approved as read (or as corrected)." If later, however, it seems that an error has unavoidably crept into the minutes, the usual procedure is to adopt a resolution expressing the fact that the error be corrected, rather than to tamper with the minutes when the memories of those who attended might not be as fresh as they were.

To expunge from the record is a motion sometimes made, but it is definitely not recommended. If one moves to expunge from the record and the motion is passed, then that section is either erased, or a piece of paper is pasted over it, or it is struck out with ink. It is very unwise to use the expunging motion, and the expunging of a part of the records should be reserved for very serious matters. As a matter of fact, from the legal viewpoint an organization is not allowed to expunge anything from a correct record of proceedings.

VI. Duties of Officers

PRESIDENT OR PRESIDING OFFICER   The most important officer of an organization is the presiding officer, who is always addressed, when presiding, by legal title. The form of address to the presiding officer is "Mister (or Madam) Chairman" or "Mister (or Madam) President." Under no circumstances does a president talk about himself in the first person. For example, if Mrs. Doe were president, she would never say "I." She might, in making a report of something that has happened outside of the group, report "your president did thus and so." However, when making a ruling at a meeting the presiding officer always speaks as "the chair," meaning the chairman or presiding officer. The president has two sets of duties: the first is to achieve the objectives for which the organization was formed; the second is to understand and use parliamentary law. *These duties do not vary in any organization.*

It is the duty of a presiding officer to be regular and prompt in attendance at meetings, to call the meetings to order at the stated time, and to preserve order. The latter is of the greatest importance. If members talk among themselves or are noisy, it is the duty of the president to call them to order, pleasantly *but firmly*. This is done by one tap of the gavel. Right here it should be emphasized that the president is expected to have a gavel with which to call the meeting to order. It is not effective to clap hands *or* to knock on a table with one's knuckles *or* to tap a water glass with a spoon. In most organizations the president must use a gavel. The chair must entertain motions that are in order, put them to a vote, repeat them, or ask the secretary to repeat them whenever requested to do so. The chair must give respectful attention to the discussion in the proper channel. The chair must announce the result of all votes and, in general, carry forward the business of the assembly to the conclusions which it desires to reach.

May we impress upon you another point about presiding? You are expected to stand while stating a motion, while putting a motion to the vote, and when declaring the results. In some very intimate groups and very small assemblies a presiding officer may remain seated, though it is not a good practice to pursue. It is not always necessary for the chair to rise in order to recognize a member; neither does the presiding officer have to stand while a question is being discussed, but it is suggested that standing often keeps the meeting under his control with a great deal more ease.

The ideal president cultivates a good voice, dignity, courtesy, tact, and absolutely impartial bearing at all times. He or she knows parliamentary law and knows when to enforce a rule and when, by unanimous consent, to show some laxity in its enforcement. The president exercises tact in order to encourage the timid member and skill in politely repressing the overly enthusiastic. The president, by the very fact of being the president, forfeits the right to make, second, or discuss a motion while presiding. The chair does not, however, forfeit the right to vote, though most presiding officers do not exercise this right. Sometimes the chair is asked if a motion is in order. The proper answer to that is "the member may make the motion and the chair will decide whether the motion is in order." It is not possible to rule on any motion unless the chair knows the exact wording of the motion.

Any special communications and certainly any formal communications sent by the organization should be signed by both the president and the secretary. If a called meeting is held, the call goes out signed by the secretary by order of the president, and it should so be stated. The call should also state the purpose of the meeting. The president generally has the power of appointing all standing committees and, usually, the power of appointing special committees. However, it is possible that the constitution and by-laws provide another means of appointing committees. An act of courtesy that not very many officers think of, but that would help tremendously, would be for the president to invite the vice-president(s), both or several if there are more than one, to preside occasionally. This given a certain amount of confidence, and certainly a lot of experience, to a vice-president, and it is generally considered to be one of the courtesies that promotes goodwill in the conduct of meetings and in the atmosphere of the organization.

VICE-PRESIDENT   It is the duty of the vice-president to preside if the president is not present, or whenever he is requested to do so by the president. The vice-president always takes the chair when the president has to step down for any reason, as explained previously. If the absence or disability of the president is permanent, the vice-president becomes the acting president with all the powers and duties of the president, but unless there is a special provision to that effect, he does not become president. When the President of the United States dies and the Vice-President assumes the office, he actually becomes President according to the provisions of the U.S. Constitution. However, such succession is not provided for in most constitutions; and in most cases where a term of office is prescribed in the organization's constitution, the fact that one has served as acting president does not take away from one the right to serve the whole prescribed time as president.

RECORDING SECRETARY   One of the most important offices of any organization is that of recording secretary. Some people feel that this office is even more important than the presidency. Certainly, this office runs the presidency a close second, because although the president is the head, the secretary is the right hand of the organization. They, of course, must be in complete harmony and work together well. Because in a great many organizations the job of secretary is so important that a person is employed at a salary to serve in that capacity, you may have heard that a secretary has no right to vote. A member who becomes secretary forfeits no rights by holding office. Before discussing the minutes (which are of vital importance), it should be said that if the secretary is absent from a meeting a secretary *pro tempore* is elected or appointed with the approval of the organization. This person is relieved of the job as soon as the secretary reappears.

Nothing in an organization is more important than the minutes or the records, because upon those records rests the entire accuracy of the history of the organization. Far too little attention is given to the writing of the minutes, to listening to the reading of the minutes, and above all to the preservation of them. Minutes may vary considerably, but there are certain fundamentals which must be included:

1. The name of the organization.
2. The kind of meeting.
   (Was it a regular meeting, a called meeting, or an annual meeting?)
3. The place where the meeting was held.
4. The date and the time when it was called to order.

Nothing is more frustrating than to look through minutes and try to find an action. If you find the action, when did it happen? If the minutes are not dated, did the action happen in November 1962, or did it happen in January 1963? (If there is no date, how can one decide?) The records should also mention the presiding officer by name and state something about the number in attendance. You do not always have to list the people who were there, but certainly you should give the approximate number.

The minutes must give a careful record of all motions stated by the presiding officer, and the manner in which they were disposed of: Were they carried, or lost, or referred to a committee, or laid on the table, or what? The fact of adjournment and the manner in which adjournment was accomplished must also be mentioned. You do not have to mention omissions, such as "no report from," except in the case of minutes. If the minutes were not read, then the fact should be stated, and the reason for the omission should be given.

The simplest way to prepare minutes is to put each motion made and each vote taken in a separate paragraph for the sake of easy reference. It is very easy to go back over the activity if the secretary will take the time to put a word of summary in the margin. For instance, if a motion was made and action taken about painting the club building and if the secretary had put a few words such as "painting the building" in the margin, then he or she could refer to that notation without any lost time.

Minutes should always be signed by the person who wrote them, and the fact that they were approved or failed to be approved must be recorded. When a presiding officer calls for the reading of the minutes it might be wise to say, "You will please listen to the reading of the minutes." This impresses upon the members of the organization their responsibility as to the accuracy of the record. It is not fair for members to listen to the reading of the minutes and then go outside and criticize the facts or omissions. If you have listened carefully and point out any mistakes, you have done your duty.

The recording secretary is also charged with the responsibility of filing or keeping reports of committees, communications, etc. There are three ways suggested to do this. First, every communication and report may be entered in full in the minutes. Of course, this is a satisfactory and complete record that is especially convenient when a loose-leaf notebook is used. However, this method does have a way of making the minutes very bulky. The second way is to file the communication or report with a number that is recorded in the minutes. For instance, you might mention that the report of the president was made and filed under number 1 for the year 1978. The vice-president's report might be number 2, and so on. These reports could be found easily, but they will, of course, require filing cases. Without filing cases, this method is impractical. The third way is to condense the report and incorporate the con-

densation in the minutes of the organization in
the words used by the secretary. This way is the
least satisfactory, because whenever one tries to
reproduce someone else's views one may slip up
on an important point.

Parliamentary rules require that the recording
secretary send notices for meetings when directed to do so by the proper authorities. For instance, a convention call is issued by the recording
secretary unless some provision is made for
someone else to do it. (In most organizations, the
corresponding secretary sends out the notices of
regular meetings.)

The recording secretary is required to call the
meeting to order when neither the president nor
any vice-president is present, presides until a
temporary chairman is elected, and keeps a record of attendance. If there is no roll call the record would be a count of the number present. At
every meeting the secretary should have a list of
the special committees that are expected to report. It is part of the secretary's duty to give to the
chairman of a committee the names of the committee members, a copy of the motion on which

the committee is to work, and any other needed information.

A recording secretary should keep at the bottom of each set of minutes a list of the items of old business that are to be considered. For instance, in the body of the minutes it is recorded that a report will be given from a committee regarding the painting of a building. The secretary makes a notation on the bottom of the minutes among the items of old business that this report will be heard. When the president reaches that part of the agenda, the secretary is asked for items of old business. The secretary reads them one by one, and the items are then acted on by the members.

TREASURER   It is the duty of the treasurer to receive and disperse money and to keep an absolutely accurate account of all money paid in, as well as all paid out. Most treasurers keep a checkbook with detailed stubs and a record of the bills, the date, and number of the check with which the bill was paid. The treasurer should always pay bills by check so that the records are complete in every instance. A wise treasurer will in all instances require that an auditor be appointed or elected. This in no way reflects on personal honesty but is just a protection for the individual so that the organization may know at all times that the books are in perfect order and the accounts balanced.

VII. Some Troublesome Motions

DIFFERENCES BETWEEN "RECONSIDERATION" AND "RESCIND"   There are important differences between reconsidering a vote and a motion to rescind. Everyone needs to know the distinction between these two terms.

RECONSIDERING A VOTE   Reconsidering a vote is a generally misunderstood motion and should have serious consideration. The motion to reconsider a vote is applicable only to a vote on a main motion or to the last vote taken if on a motion other than a main motion. A motion to reconsider can be made only by a member who voted on the winning side, except in cases where the vote was secret, at which time any member may move to reconsider. It takes a majority vote to pass. The motion to reconsider, if carried, annuls the vote already taken and brings the original motion before the assembly again for reconsideration. It does not bring about the opposite of the vote taken.

For instance, suppose that we had voted to spend $500 to paint a building, and someone who voted on the winning side moved to reconsider the vote. The motion to reconsider was brought to a vote and was passed. That does not mean that the motion to paint is lost and that we will not spend $500. All that it means is that the matter is now again open for discussion and re-voting. This motion can only be made at the session at which the vote was taken unless a special rule extends the time.

Organizations that have meetings on consecutive days generally limit reconsideration to the day following that on which the vote was taken. (A rule very generally adopted is that a motion to reconsider a vote shall only be allowed at the same or first subsequent meeting after the vote was taken.) Sometimes a move to reconsider carries a

time limit. If that is true, then a treasurer will
certainly not pay out money, and the president
and secretary will not sign a contract. In other
words, no one will transact any business regarding that particular motion until the time during
which a reconsideration of the vote ordering such
action is possible. It is obvious that an officer could
get into serious trouble by taking any action still
under reconsideration.

No vote can be reconsidered more than once,
but if upon reconsideration the form is changed
by an amendment, then the amended motion may
be reconsidered over and over again. A vote is
sometimes reconsidered immediately after a
winning action for the express purpose of making further reconsiderations impossible. This is
known in legislative parlance as "the clincher"
and is used in parliamentary procedure of legislatures or congresses so that the matter cannot
be reopened. Blocking such an attempt to reopen
is called "applying the parliamentary clincher."

MOTION TO RESCIND   A motion to rescind is
used in order to cancel action that has been taken.
It is a main motion and *is* debatable. If previous
notice has been given that the motion to rescind

will be brought up, then the passage takes a simple majority vote; otherwise it takes a two-thirds vote to pass. It is not necessary for the maker of a motion to rescind to have been on the winning side, or is the motion to rescind in order at the same meeting at which the original motion was passed. When it is too late to have a motion to reconsider, then a motion to rescind may be in order.

One may move to rescind any action, no matter how old it is, except where an action which cannot be undone has been performed. This would apply to an action where the treasurer had paid out money which was authorized; for example, when a member had gone to a meeting as the authorized delegate of the organization.

The motion to rescind, if carried, annuls the vote already taken and brings the original motion before the group as if it had not been voted upon at all.

For example, if the motion to spend $500 for the painting of a building had been passed, but no contract had been issued, and a member wanted to have "another try at the question of whether to paint or not to paint," it would be in order to *reconsider* the vote at the *same meeting* at which the original motion was carried, but the motion would have to be to *rescind* action if made at any subsequent meeting.

SUSPENSION OF A RULE   No organization has the right to suspend the provisions of its constitution or articles of its association except by procedures spelled out in its constitution or articles. The most familiar example of required procedures is amendment of the U.S. Constitution. However, rules embodied in the by-laws may be suspended under certain conditions, and efforts to suspend such rules often occur in many organizations. In such cases, the motion may be made that we suspend *a particular rule*, but never can suspension be included in a *general* motion, because suspensions are prohibited unless prior provisions have been made and prior notice has been given that the matter will be brought up. Passage of a suspension always requires a two-thirds vote.

But remember, we cannot suspend the rule that amendments to the constitution can be made only after due notice. Neither can we suspend a rule that was made by a higher authority, such as a national or state organization of which our club is a subordinate unit.

WITHDRAWAL OF A MOTION   Another thing which is sometimes bothersome is the withdrawal of a motion. The motion to allow the withdrawal of a motion may be made by any member. If, for example, Mrs. Johnson is the person who made the original motion, she rises, addresses the chair and says, "I ask leave to withdraw my motion." Whereupon, the chair says "If there is no objection, the member is allowed to withdraw the motion." (This is a vote by "silent consent.") If any objection is made, the question of allowing withdrawal must be voted upon as any other motion. A motion cannot be withdrawn after the vote upon it has been ordered.

Any member has the right to withdraw his or her motion before it becomes the property of the assembly, that is, before it has been formally stated by the chair. An important matter in regard to withdrawal is that a member may withdraw the name of one whom he or she has nominated, and one who has been nominated may withdraw his or her own name. In other words, you cannot insist upon a vote on a name if the person who is being voted upon does not wish to have the vote taken.

Points of Order   No assembly can transact its business unless order is maintained. The prime duty of a presiding officer is to establish and maintain order. This applies not only to parliamentary procedure but to the behavior of the members as well. The chair is at liberty to suspend business if it is considered necessary. The chair may interrupt a member who is speaking, if in the presiding officer's opinion, the member is out of order, or if the chair wishes the member to cease speaking until the rest of the assembly is brought to order. On the other hand, if the presiding officer does not conduct the business of the organization as the assembly thinks it should be conducted, any member has the privilege to raise a point of order. It must be raised at the time of action, that is, when the officer makes an incorrect ruling or when he has overstepped the bounds of parliamentary procedure. If it is not made at this time, it may not be made at all.

The form in which this is done is as follows:

The member rises, addresses the chair, and without waiting for recognition, says "I rise to a point of order." Any member who has the floor when a point of order is raised, if he understands the etiquette of parliamentary procedure, will sit down instantly. The chair then says, "The member will please state the point of order." The member must then make a clear, brief statement of what in his opinion is unparliamentary. He should be very sure to make a point. He can't simply say, generally, "I don't think the presiding officer is fair." He must specifically state in what way he considers the presiding officer has failed to carry out the correct parliamentary procedure. The presiding officer must make a decision. If the chair agrees that the point is correct, he says so, in the words, "the point is well taken." If he doesn't agree he may say, "the point is not well taken," and give the reasons for the decision. Before deciding, the chair may ask for any information he wishes, or he may refer the question of order at once to the assembly for a vote.

If the presiding officer states his decision, and that is not the voice or the feeling of the assembly, any member may make an appeal by rising and saying, "Mr. (or Madam) Chairman, I appeal the decision of the chair." This is an appeal from the decision of the chair to a higher authority. The highest authority is always—in all matters— the assembly itself. If the appeal is seconded by a member, then it must be voted upon. The presiding officer rises, states the reasons for the decision given, even when the appeal is undebatable. He does not leave the chair to make such a statement. In taking the vote, the presiding officer says, "The decision of the chair is appealed from. Shall the chair's decision be sustained." A majority vote is necessary for sustaining the chair. A tie actually sustains the chair, and the chair may vote to make it a tie. The vote is "yes" if the ruling of the chair is sustained.

When the question of order is finally disposed of either by the chair or the assembly, business is resumed exactly where it was interrupted. If the question of order that was raised was decided "well taken," the change is made at once. If a member was speaking when the question of order was raised, that member has the right to resume as soon as the question is settled, unless the point of order was that that particular member had already used up more than the time allowed and the ruling of the chair was sustained.

In other words, the chair's decision is questioned. If he agrees that he has acted incorrectly he so states and the matter is adjusted. If, on the other hand, he declares that he has not acted incorrectly, and rules that the point of order is not well taken, someone may move that the chair's action be upheld or that it not be upheld, and a vote is taken. The vote decides whether or not the chair shall be upheld in the decision. We do not often have appeals from the ruling of the chair in small organizations, but it is a fairly common occurrence in large legislative or congressional groups.

DIVISION OF THE QUESTION   If a motion is put before the body and someone feels that it should be acted upon section by section for clarification, the member may move that the question be divided. He must state in the motion exactly how he wishes the matter divided. If the motion to divide is passed, that does not mean that the original motion or any part of it is passed. It means only that the parts will be considered separately. Each section is then treated as a main motion.

Robert says: "Division of the question is really an amendment and subject to the same rule."

OBJECTION TO CONSIDERATION   If a motion is made by any member who wishes to object to the consideration of a main motion, no second is required, and the motion is not debatable or amendable, and passage requires a two-thirds vote. The form of the motion is "I object to the consideration of the question." The chair puts the motion: "Shall the question be considered?" If there is a two-thirds vote against consideration, the motion objected to is not considered at this time.

DIVISION OF THE ASSEMBLY   When the chair announces the results of a vote and someone doubts its accuracy, the member may rise and state that he doubts the accuracy of the vote as announced by the chair. The vote may be repeated, or the chair or the member may call for a division of the assembly. The chair then asks that all those in favor stand and the votes are counted. Then the chair calls for those against to stand, and the same procedure is followed. The chair then announces the recounted vote, and says whether the motion is carried or lost.

VIII. Nominations and Elections

NOMINATIONS   Nominations may be made by any member and are allowed even though nominations may have been made by a committee, unless a by-law or standing rule or resolution restricts nomination to the committee. If a presiding officer is asking for nominations for an office, and a nominating committee has been appointed, it is generally the rule that the presiding officer ask for a report from the nominating committee. Then he must ask, "Are there nominations from the floor?" If there are no nominations from the floor, the nominee who has been presented by the nominating committee is generally the one who will be elected. Sometimes there are several nominations from the floor.

A motion to close nominations, if carried, cuts off all further nominations. This is generally not a popular move, because people feel that they are being squelched. However, if the nominations have been made and it is moved and seconded to close the nominations, then the chair immediately puts the motion in this form: "It has been moved and seconded that nominations be closed. All in favor please say 'aye', opposed 'no'. The 'ayes' have it and nominations are closed."

The thing to remember is that if there is only one person nominated for a position, then that person is the candidate. Even if there is only one candidate for an office, a vote must be taken if the election is to be legal. The chair must declare the election of Mr. or Mrs. Brown or the election has not been finished. A word of warning seems in order: nomination, or "the act of proposing for an office" is NOT ELECTION. When the members of a nominating committee approach a member they are saying, "May we propose your name for such and such an office? If you are elected, will you serve?" The nominating committee has no power to guarantee the election of a nominee. A wise nominee will keep quiet about having been approached by the committee until the election has taken place. There will be fewer hurt feelings in that case.

The nominating committee is not the electing body. If they were, that would be tantamount to turning over to three or five members of a committee, the power of electing all officers. We must never lose sight of the fact that any member has the right to nominate or "name" a candidate for office. Nominations do *not* require a second, and it is the duty of the chair to call for nominations from the floor in order to be sure that nothing is railroaded through.

Of course there are other forms for nominations. There is the form for nominating that is called "nominations by ballot," which consists of having little slips of paper passed so that each member may write in the name of the person he wishes to nominate for a position. It is generally considered the proper form to take the two receiving the greatest number of votes, declare them the nominees, and hold an election between those two. In most organizations it is very unwise to nominate people who have not agreed to serve if elected, because a very embarrassing situation can arise when the elected officer says he is in no position to serve. We should always consult the person whose name is going to be presented and find out whether he is willing to assume the responsibility.

VOTING   Of course voting may be either by secret ballot, or writing in the name, or by what is called voting by voice. If there is a question in the mind of the presiding officer as to the outcome of a voice vote, the chair simply asks the secretary to count the votes, or asks the group who vote in favor to stand. Then after they are counted, the negative vote stands and they are counted. If you are voting by ballot, it is necessary to have tellers who will collect and count the ballots. Tellers may be used in any form of voting.

There are several ways of voting and it might be well to consider them here. Elections are won by a majority vote, by a plurality, or by a two-thirds vote.

MAJORITY VOTES   By majority vote is meant a majority—more than half—of all votes cast. By special provision it may mean a majority of the entire membership or a majority of those present.

Suppose a society has 100 members. The smallest number according to parliamentary law which can transact business is then 51, except if a different quorum is set by the constitution. Suppose then only 51 members attended the meeting. A motion, which by special provision required a majority vote of the entire membership, would be lost even if 50 persons voted for it. A motion under which a special provision required a majority vote of those present would be carried if only 26 voted for it. A motion which required only a majority vote would be passed if only 1 person voted in favor of it, providing no one voted against it. (That is a majority vote, so that it must be clearly understood whether the vote may be carried by majority of those present or by a majority of the entire membership.)

PLURALITY VOTES Plurality means the greatest of three or more numbers. In election it means the number by which the vote cast for the candidate who receives the greatest number exceeds the vote cast for the candidate who receives the next greatest number, when there are more than two candidates. To illustrate the difference between a majority and a plurality vote, suppose that 100 legal votes were cast. If a majority of all votes cast were to constitute an election, there would be no election until one candidate received at least 51 votes. If a plurality vote constituted an election, it would be possible for each one of 98 candidates to receive one vote and the one candidate to be elected by receiving two votes.

TWO-THIRDS VOTES A two-thirds vote simply means that twice as many members vote on one side as on the other.

TIE VOTES A tie vote occurs when an equal number vote in the affirmative and in the negative. The motion is declared lost on the principle that it requires at least a majority to carry a motion. The only exception to this rule is that a tie vote on an appeal sustains the chair. The chair may vote on any matter upon which he wishes to vote. However, it is not customary for the chair to vote except when the vote is by ballot or roll call, or when his vote would break a tie. The chair is not compelled to vote even to break a tie.

IX. Order of Business

I t is very important that every presiding officer have a clearly worked out order of business. This is usually done by having the president write out an agenda. As each matter of business is attended to, he takes a pencil and strikes through that item of the agenda, which is a signal to go on to the next matter. If he wishes, he may write in the margin of his order of business what action was taken regarding each matter. This is a very helpful system when checking the results of a meeting. The first thing is the call to order and establishing the fact that a quorum is present. The minutes of the preceding meeting, or of any meeting which has been held since the last minutes were presented, are then called for and they are read by the recording secretary. At any meeting one set of minutes must be approved before another can be presented.

If there is a special order of business for which the meeting was called, then the special order is called for. If a special order of business is set, nothing may interfere with it. For instance, if the adopted order of business calls for the election of officers at eleven o'clock of the second day of a convention, no matter what business is considered by the organization it must be suspended and exactly on the stroke of eleven the special order of electing officers must be entered into. This is exceedingly important and must be remembered by all presiding officers.

After any special order of business is finished, communications from the president are heard and acted upon. Then come the reports of officers, usually beginning with the vice-president, followed by the secretaries, and finishing with the treasurer. Then the reports of committees are heard, although it is not necessary to hear every committee report at every meeting. The president, after consultation with the committee chairmen, predetermines the committees that will report. The chair should know whether or not there is any unfinished business; the presiding officer should not have to ask the membership. The chair announces that there are items of unfinished business, proceeds to state them one at a time, and they are acted upon. Then new business, or sometimes it is called miscellaneous business, is called for, which gives an opportunity for the introduction and transaction of any business that has not yet been called for. At this time the recommendations of the board and committees may be heard and the necessary action be taken.

Order of exercises at an annual meeting are slightly different from those at a regular meeting. The place for communications from the president is usually immediately after the approval of the minutes and before the reports of the other officers. However, at an annual meeting, when the president makes a formal address, the place of honor seems to be after the reports of all the other officers have been heard. At the annual meeting of an organization, minutes of the preceding annual meeting may be read and approved. Some organizations which have two or three day sessions require the secretary to have minutes for one day ready to read at the beginning session of the following day.

The accounts of the treasurer should always be audited before the annual report is presented, and there should be a sufficient interval of time be-

tween the close of a fiscal year and the date of the
annual meeting to make this possible. If the accounts have not been audited it is quite good form
to have a motion to refer them to an auditor. When
an organization holds an annual meeting or a
convention of one or more days, it is generally the
rule that a printed program is prepared, which is
followed except when the assembly votes a
change in the order of business.

X. Helpful Suggestions

A SIMPLE MOTION FROM BEGINNING TO END

1. Rise and address the chair.
2. State your name for the secretary to record.
3. Be recognized by the chair, then you have
   the floor.
4. State motion ("I move that" or "I move to").
5. Be seated while chair calls for a second.
6. Motion is seconded.
7. Motion is stated by chair.

8. Motion is discussed.
9. Chair calls for the votes, for and against.
10. Chair declares result of vote and what happens as result of vote.

WHAT TO INCLUDE IN THE MINUTES

Name of organization
Date: day, month, year
Place of meeting
Time
Type of meeting (whether regular, called, convention, etc.)
Approximate number in attendance
Who presided
All business (including approval of minutes, summary of treasurer's report and committee reports)
Motions: name of maker (name of seconder, if desired)
Each step in carrying through motion, i.e., amendments, etc.
Ultimate decision on motion (carried or lost)
Time of adjournment
Signature of secretary

At bottom of minutes list pending or unfinished business

Minutes must be kept in permanent form as they are legal evidence of what transpired and make up the history of the organization.

CONSTITUTION, BY-LAWS, AND STANDING RULES
An organization should adopt a constitution, a set of by-laws, and some standing rules as soon after it is formed as is practical. The constitution should be more difficult to amend than the by-laws, and should thus contain only those items which are fundamental to the organization. The by-laws should list those details which may be changed without upsetting the entire balance of the club. Standing rules should contain such rules as may be passed without previous notice by a majority vote at any meeting, and thus may be suspended by a majority vote. Changes in the constitution and by-laws should be after previous notice and be made by a two-thirds vote. There is such great variation in constitutions, by-laws, and standing rules that no effort will be made here to outline what they should contain. It is suggested that

those who are writing such documents consult a recognized book on parliamentary law, secure a copy of a model constitution, or secure the aid of an experienced parliamentarian. Often the success or failure of a club is dependent upon the safeguards thrown around it by its constitution and by-laws.

WAYS OF VOTING There are several ways in which to vote. The one most generally used is viva voce vote (calling for the ayes and nays, or yes and no.) A roll call may be used, hands may be raised, a division of the house may be called, and the members register their vote by standing. Then there is a ballot or secret written vote, which is considered the most parliamentary form of vote generally used. Some organizations allow vote by mail or by proxy, but such means must be prescribed in the constitution or by-laws.

There is a generally misunderstood method of voting—that of voting by general consent. The chair may say something like this: "If there is no objection, the report will be accepted as information." If no one says anything, then the group has voted by silence or by general consent. Such a vote is frequently taken when an agenda is finished, and the chair wants to adjourn a meeting expeditiously.

A member has the right to change his vote up to the time that the vote has been announced, unless the vote was by written ballot.

Who counts the vote? The chair may count the vote, may ask the secretary, or appoint tellers to do so. If tellers are used, they read the result. It is then handed to the chair, who *officially announces* the result of the vote. The tellers determine whether the vote is a majority vote or not. If it is a majority vote, they state that a certain candidate has received a majority of votes and has been elected. The chair then announces that that candidate has been elected to the specific office.

Motions According to
Parliamentary Procedure

(Except where indicated, all of the following motions require a second, may be debated, amended, reconsidered and require a majority vote.)

1. Accept report: not amendable
2. Adjourn: not amendable, not debatable, cannot be reconsidered, no quorum necessary
3. Adjourn to specific time: not debatable, cannot be reconsidered, no quorum necessary
4. Adopt orders of the day: not amendable, no debate, does not require chair's recognition, cannot be reconsidered, no second necessary
5. Adopt report: can be committed
6. Amend a motion: can be committed, limited debate
7. Amend constitution: can be committed, limited debate

8. Amend minutes: can be committed, limited debate

9. Amend motion to amend: not amendable, can be committed, limited debate

10. Appeal: not amendable, does not require chair's recognition, limited debate, cannot be reconsidered

11. Approve minutes: can be committed, limited debate

12. Call to order while debatable question pending: not amendable, limited debate, does not require chair's recognition, no second necessary

13. Call to order while nondebatable question pending: not amendable, not debatable, does not require chair's recognition, no second necessary

14. Close debate: not amendable, not debatable, requires two-thirds vote

15. Commit

16. Consider out of order: not amendable, not debatable, requires two-thirds vote

17. Consider special order: limited debate, requires two-thirds vote

18. Divide question: not debatable, cannot be reconsidered, no second necessary

19. Enter in minutes: not amendable, limited debate

20. Extend time for debate: not debatable

21. Fix time and place of meeting: no quorum necessary

22. Fix time or place to which to adjourn

23. Lay on the table: not amendable, not debatable

24. Limit debate: not debatable, requires two-thirds vote

25. Make nominations: not amendable, cannot be reconsidered, no second necessary

26. Move the previous question: not amendable, not debatable, requires two-thirds vote

27. Object to consideration: not amendable, not debatable, does not require chair's recognition

28. Place on file: not amendable, limited debate

29. Postpone indefinitely: not amendable
30. Postpone to definite time: limited debate
31. Provide manner of voting: limited debate
32. Question after the previous question: not amendable, not debatable, does not require chair's recognition, no second necessary
33. Read papers not under consideration: not amendable, not debatable
34. Read papers under consideration: not amendable, not debatable, no second necessary
35. Receive: not amendable, not debatable
36. Recess: not debatable, no quorum necessary, cannot be reconsidered
37. Recommit
38. Reconsider debatable motion: not amendable, cannot be reconsidered
39. Reconsider undebatable motion: not amendable, not debatable, cannot be reconsidered
40. Refer
41. Rescind: not amendable, can be committed

42. Rise: not amendable, not debatable, no quorum necessary, cannot be reconsidered

43. Strike out and insert: can be committed, limited debate

44. Substitute: can be committed, limited debate

45. Suspend rule: not amendable, not debatable, cannot be reconsidered, requires two-thirds vote

46. Table or take from table: not amendable, not debatable

47. Withdraw motion: not amendable, not debatable, no second necessary

Summary

of Actions on Motions

Motions that are not amendable

Accept a report
Adjourn or rise
Amend a motion to amend
Appeal
Close nominations
Consider question out of proper order
Enter in minutes
Lay on the table
Leave to speak out of order
Make nominations
Object to consideration
Adopt orders of the day

Place on file
Raise point of order
Postpone indefinitely
Raise previous question
Raise question of privilege
Receive
Reconsider a vote
Suspend a rule
Take from the table
Withdraw a motion

Motions that may be made
while another has the floor

∽

Appeal decision of chair
Object to consideration
Adopt orders of the day
Raise point of order
Raise question of personal privilege
Reconsider and enter in the minutes

Motions that are not debatable

Adjourn, rise, or take a recess
Appeal
Close nominations
Consider question out of order
Divide the question
Extend, limit, or close debate
Fix time or place to which to adjourn
Go into executive session
Lay on the table
Leave to speak out of order
Object to consideration
Call for orders of the day
Raise point of order
Raise previous question
Raise question of privilege
Read papers
Receive a report

Reconsider the vote on an undebatable motion
Suspend a rule
Take from the table
Withdraw a motion

∽

Motions that require no second

Divide the question
Make nominations
Object to consideration
Adopt orders of the day
Raise point of order
Raise question of privilege
Read papers under consideration
Adopt board or committee recommendations

Motions that require a two-thirds vote

Amend or suspend rule
Close nominations
Consider question out of order
Extend, limit, or close debate
Make a special order
Object to consideration
Raise previous question
Rescind, if no previous notice

Motions that cannot be reconsidered

Adjourn to specified time

Adjourn or rise

Any motion which has already gone into effect

Appeal

Call for orders of day

Divide question

Lay on table if affirmative

Make nominations

Object to consideration

Raise previous question (after any vote affected by it has been taken)

Recess

Reconsider

Take from table, if affirmative

INDEX